T0023677

FCK OFF, HOLIDAYS, I'M COLORING

'Tis the Season for Curse-Filled Coloring Pages

DARE YOU

STAMP CO.

A belligerent subset of
Cider Mill Press Book Publishers

Illustrations by Lizzie Preston

CIDER MILL
PRESS

BOOK
PUBLISHERS
KENNEBUNKPORT, MAINE

Fuck Off, Holidays, I'm Coloring

Copyright © 2022 by Appleseed Press Book Publishers LLC.

This is an officially licensed book by Cider Mill Press Book Publishers LLC.

All rights reserved under the Pan-American and International Copyright Conventions.

No part of this book may be reproduced in whole or in part, scanned, photocopied, recorded, distributed in any printed or electronic form, or reproduced in any manner whatsoever, or by any information storage and retrieval system now known or hereafter invented, without express written permission of the publisher, except in the case of brief quotations embodied in critical articles and reviews.

The scanning, uploading, and distribution of this book via the internet or via any other means without permission of the publisher is illegal and punishable by law. Please support authors' rights, and do not participate in or encourage piracy of copyrighted materials.

13-Digit ISBN: 978-1-64643-290-5
10-Digit ISBN: 1-64643-290-8

This book may be ordered by mail from the publisher. Please include $5.99 for postage and handling. Please support your local bookseller first!

Books published by Cider Mill Press Book Publishers are available at special discounts for bulk purchases in the United States by corporations, institutions, and other organizations. For more information, please contact the publisher.

Cider Mill Press Book Publishers
"Where Good Books Are Ready for Press"
PO Box 454
12 Spring Street
Kennebunkport, Maine 04046

Visit us online!
cidermillpress.com

Printed in China

Typography: Adobe Garamond Pro, Archive Tilt, Festivo Letters, Satisfy

1 2 3 4 5 6 7 8 9 0

IF you're reading this, you're our kind of motherfucker. Or you just might be a fan of Dare You Stamp Co. already. And why wouldn't you be? We're awesome. Our line of completely irreverent products is perfect for sticking it to the man and flipping off your haters with style.

Whether you signed your vacation request with our *F This Shit Stamp Kit*, told Santa where he can shove his coal with our *Tis the Season to Be Naughty Postcards*, or became the antihero of your dreams with our *POW! Stamp Kit*, you know we're done being polite. So why not tell the world to fuck off? Break out that pack of crayons you abandoned in middle school and color the fuck out of any number of these swear-filled pages. Frame them, hang them, or leave them all over your boss's desk with your resignation letter stapled to the back. What you do with these are up to you, dumbass. If you feel like showing off, you can tag @cidermillpress on social media and share your fucking awesome creations with the hashtag #fuckoffimcoloring.

Now go forth and be the complete asshole you were meant to be, we dare you.

TABLE *of* CONTENTS

INTRODUCTION

Forced good tidings, carb-filled family gatherings, boring work parties, crappy presents—the holiday season can be a real drag. Don't let societal obligations get you down. Skip the BS and keep cozy and entertained at home with this curse-filled coloring book! Avoid the annoying crowds, family, and friends and do the holiday season however the hell you want.

You don't need to spend all of that money, eat all of that crap, or pretend that you care. Sick and tired of all the holiday cards that clog your mailbox and then go straight into the trash? Let people know how you really feel by coloring one of these randy pages and then sending it their way. Or leave one out for St. Nick, that creep.

Tell the Holidaze stress to fuck off and turn ho, ho, ho, into a ha, ha, ha!

HAPPY
HOLIDAZE

.

BAH HUMBUG

UP TO
SNOW GOOD

COAL FOR
BRAINS

FUCK
BEING GOOD

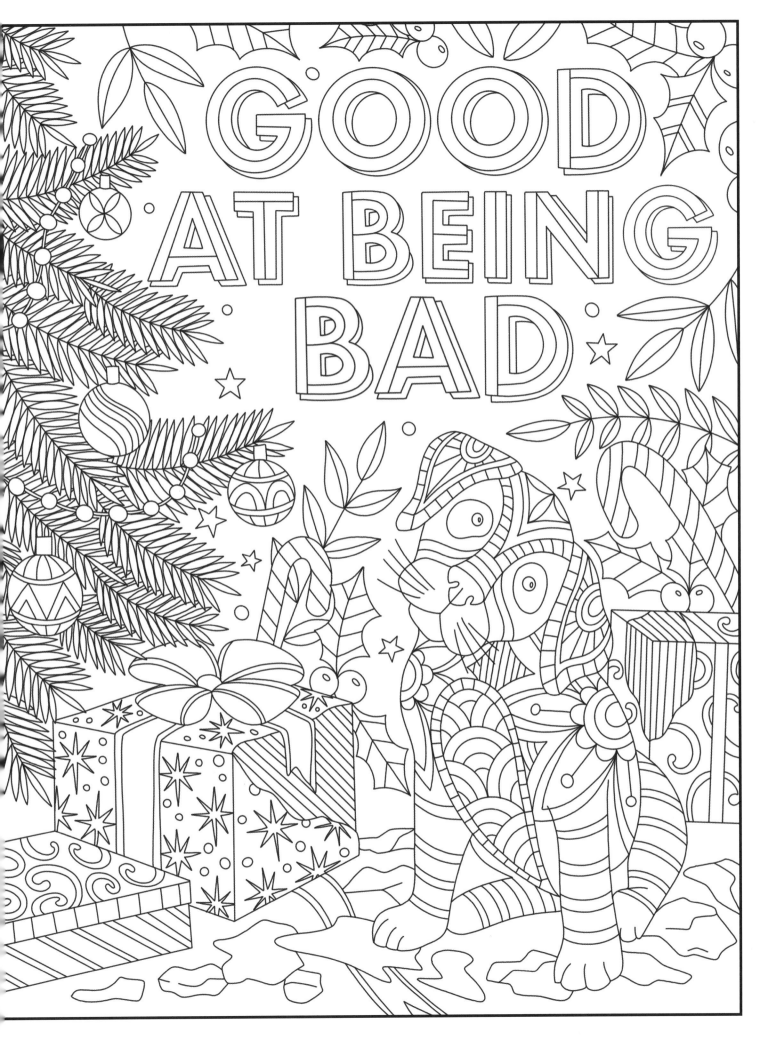

#FUCKOFFIMCOLORING #FUCKOFFIMCOLORING
#FUCKOFFIMCOLORING #FUCKOFFIMCOLORING
#FUCKOFFIMCOLORING #FUCKOFFIMCOLORING
#FUCKOFFIMCOLORING #FUCKOFFIMCOLORING
#FUCKOFFIMCOLORING #FUCKOFFIMCOLORING
#FUCKOFFIMCOLORING #FUCKOFFIMCOLORING
#FUCKOFFIMCOLORING #FUCKOFFIMCOLORING
#FUCKOFFIMCOLORING #FUCKOFFIMCOLORING
#FUCKOFFIMCOLORING #FUCKOFFIMCOLORING
#FUCKOFFIMCOLORING #FUCKOFFIMCOLORING
#FUCKOFFIMCOLORING #FUCKOFFIMCOLORING
#FUCKOFFIMCOLORING #FUCKOFFIMCOLORING
#FUCKOFFIMCOLORING #FUCKOFFIMCOLORING
#FUCKOFFIMCOLORING #FUCKOFFIMCOLORING
#FUCKOFFIMCOLORING #FUCKOFFIMCOLORING
#FUCKOFFIMCOLORING #FUCKOFFIMCOLORING
#FUCKOFFIMCOLORING #FUCKOFFIMCOLORING
#FUCKOFFIMCOLORING #FUCKOFFIMCOLORING
#FUCKOFFIMCOLORING #FUCKOFFIMCOLORING
#FUCKOFFIMCOLORING

SHARE YOUR BITCHIN' MASTERPIECES

Don't keep your colorful creations
to yourself—take a pic and share it
on social media with the hashtag
#fuckoffimcoloring and tag us
@cidermillpress!

For more stress-relieving coloring, check out:

Fuck Off, I'm Coloring

Fuck Off, I'm Still Coloring

Fuck Off, I Can't Stop Coloring

Fuck Off, Coronavirus, I'm Coloring

Bite Me, I'm Coloring

Available now!

INDEX

ABOUT
CIDER MILL PRESS
BOOK PUBLISHERS

Good ideas ripen with time. From seed to harvest,
Cider Mill Press brings fine reading, information, and
entertainment together between the covers of its creatively
crafted books. Our Cider Mill bears fruit twice a year,
publishing a new crop of titles each spring and fall.

"Where Good Books Are Ready for Press"

Visit us online at
cidermillpress.com
or write to us at
PO Box 454
12 Spring St.
Kennebunkport, Maine 04046